Things left unsaid

Prose from a therapist's playground

Steven Eserin

Gestalt psychotherapist

Dedication

To my boys, who are undeniably, the best part of
me.

May your days be filled with just enough
madness to keep you sane.

Themes

Introduction

I'm no writer, not in the traditional sense; and
this is not an apology. My education did not
prepare me for a literary life. I have dyslexia.
That's a hindrance of epic proportions. But, and
a big but, I love words. I have ideas, and things
to say, which are at times worth hearing, if you
take the time and look past the poor grammar
and the lack of training, there may be
something for you here. We might struggle to
call them poems, maybe if you ignore the total
lack of structure, metre and technical know-how;
Read between the words, see what you find.

In psychotherapy we search our deepest places,
we uncover our fears, explore our shadows, hopes,
dreams, and loves; Both great and small, our love
for those we have lost and those we hold dear. It
is a powerful emotive thing, to sit and bear
witness to another's pain, sorrow, fears, joy and
dreams. To allow all these to speak to our own.
And, to see the person who emerges at the end is
an unspeakable privilege for which I am ever
grateful.

One remarkable aspect of these pieces of prose is that each time I read them I am transported back to the moments which inspired them, the words of people I have met, the thoughts inspired in me, those points of exquisite contact when I understood the person opposite me, or I understood more clearly those parts of myself I had hidden from my own sight.

I'm a psychotherapist, so words are the medium through which I swim. Daily, we push around ideas, look for strong places in the psyche to shore up with stronger foundations and hunt down neurosis to prod until they dissolve. We look for the authentic person who has been hiding all along under the roles played, and then we support its coming to the light.

I only have words, the acts of listening, understanding, and attempting to help you grasp the here-and-now phenomenological experience of being human. I am a mirror, though imperfect, I reflect people back to themselves through the art of exploring the obvious.

Sometimes, it is not as obvious as we might imagine. So, after each client leaves, when I sit to write my clinical notes, there are times when the patterns of interaction, the process running underneath elude me. And often, to help me coalesce the disparate concepts, I write poems, thoughts or ideas, about our experience, my experience of my client and our relationship, and the themes we struggled with. Or I may choose to write because the experience we shared was astonishing, inspirational, and too good to let go without marking in some way. Some of this prose is about my own therapeutic journey, which is long, not to mention, ongoing; And it is no understatement to add, it has led me on a most glorious path of discovery.

I write from the perspective of a therapist, and occasionally I sit in the client's space after they have left the room; in an attempt to embody what I have seen. Then I might write from my imagined version of the client's view, its fantasy mostly, also projection, and counter-transference too. Often I find I have returned the next week with insights that would previously have been lost. These moments are usually expressed in a semi-poetic form.

Above all, I write because I love to, despite my
dyslexia. Writing poetry helps me comprehend
abstractions which would be unknowable or
possibly indescribable through other mediums.
This process is complicated for me because I
tend to think in pictures, which I translate
into words. Part of my dyslexia I guess. It's
always been the way for me, it's a blessing
really. Often I will see played out a short
abstract movie in my head, it will be like a
moving surrealist picture. Usually, it will
contain an existential message about the work I
am doing and what is going on between me and
the client; And, if I turn these images into
poetry, something happens in the translation.
Like a child looking at something for the first
time and really seeing it. As though I witness
wisdom as it gracefully unfolds before me.

Occasionally between sessions I will sit and
allow my mind to free-roam, to create an image
which represents the relationship between me
and a client I have in mind. Almost without fail
this gives me insight into where we are not
meeting, or how my perception of clients is
skewed by my own experience. When I convert

these images to prose, things can get a little weird. But hey, I would hardly describe myself as "normal". Whatever that is.

It is a vast honour for me to bear witness to the stories people share with me; To witness the love they share and the pain of separation or love lost. I meet the most amazing people, and on rare occasions, people so extraordinary I feel I will never forget them.

Splitting these bits of writing into themes has been difficult, I chose 4 main themes but there is considerable crossover between them. Not an easy choice, between connection and love, or the void created by a lack of being seen and understood Vs grief. With so many interwoven patterns of behaviour and thought, the definitions become confluent, with boundaries indistinct.

Enjoy.

Love and loss, sadness and grief.

This is one theme which is a constant. In therapy, the vast majority of complaints brought by clients stem from loss. There is no getting away from our need for love or its twin, sadness. Grief is evident in every session, love lost, dreams shattered, parts of ourselves that seem to have died, and potential has gone unrealised. It is an endless well, from which we must drink deeply if we are to grow. To know sadness is to know love, and to know love is to know we live.

Breathe

I recall the first time
Your soul breathed that soundless word to mine.
Every moment since
I hold a barely disguised longing
To hear it whisper my name.
But you are silence.
And I am grief.

Her love

Her love was a beautiful thing
That seemed to have a life all its own.
She regularly showed love
to the people who hurt her most.
Though she gave up long ago
Expecting them to be anything other than what
they were.
Anticipating only drama.
And as they rejected her again and again
through the smallest slights
She accepted the inevitability
And gave her love to herself instead.

Essence

When I heard your essence speak
I fell,
Bewitched.
I had no choice
I could no more resist
Than I could have flown to the moon.
I have been searching for you
ever since.
Every face in the crowd scanned
every passing car
pedestrians scrutinised.
All in the hope of a glimpse of you

Beautiful Torment

I might be tormented
But rather this
Than to have never heard your voice,
Been transfixed by your laugh,
Or breathed in unison with you.
Your absence is a beautiful pain.
But in those moments at least, I can say...
I lived.

Breaking

I let my heart break when you left
I could have worn a mask
Duck taped over bloody fissures
with hopeful platitudes
Smiles that would never reach my eyes.
Cover the pain with hedonism
Run from my dis-ease
Into the arms of another
And another
And another.

instead, I sat;
Clutched at the pain lurching in my chest.
Clawed arthritic fingers grasping
to contain the spasms
Of searing cold heat..

And I breathed.
Cried until I was dry;
On the inside at least.

Finally, I said goodbye.
Smiled at the memory of your Smile
Your sharp wit

The recollection of the moment
When my soul first met yours.
And, in the going through,
the pieces came back together.
No effort
No struggle
I just felt them into place.

Voice

Today I wore the memory of your voice.
Of when it had played across my soul
Making my heart skip.
I wore it like an exquisite velvet cloak.
To shelter me from the storms.

what of love?

I needed to meet you.
Before I stepped into love.
Well,
I'm not sure I even remember clearly
But now some certainty from feeling;
Safety and vulnerability
held in synchronous union.

What of love?
More than transference?
More than hormonal psychotropic drug-hazed
madness?

I want to cut you from my mind
Kill this pain of never having
Knowing you were never mine to have.
To no longer feel this madness of wanting
and not wanting.

You were a beautiful and terrible lesson.

The first and the last

Know that you are
the last thought before sleep
the first image upon waking.
The words waiting behind my thoughts
for each moment of inactivity,
To spill forth.
A beautiful riot of colour
Upon the screen of my mind.

Impossible

I thought it impossible
to hold two in such high regard simultaneously.
to adore one and cherish another.
without reducing the first, or limiting the
second.
Though complications constrain me
and the second call goes unanswered
still, the call is heard in my deepest places
and I do not retreat from its strength
only its promise of pain.

The difference between
and, the respect offered
by distance
and silence.
But, it seems torturous still,
to concede I am smitten and can never act
for fear of destroying all that I love.

Beautiful madness

You are a beautiful kind of crazy.
The kind of crazy that keeps me up at night
Hoping to see you tomorrow
Like the breath I need to take;
But hold instead, knowing I must first breathe
out.

Sunrise

I am the night waiting for sunrise;
Burned away by your light,
the moment you awake.

I am the ice;
Melting to the touch of your warmth.
Becoming liquid before your fingertips.

Between

I don't believe in true love

You mean you have not experienced it? Or it just doesn't exist.

I want it to be real, true.

I hope one day you have a love who notices the space created when you leave a room. And longs for you to fill it again.

I can't imagine that...

That you deserve it? Or that it might exist?

Either...

I think I did

I did love her.
I think...
The sound of her name
Carried on another's voice,
would arrest my heart with longing.

And my waking moments were filled
with the memory of my lips
in the crook of her hips;
ear, warm against her rumbling belly.

Maybe I loved what she gave me?
That safe feeling.
The contentment in normality
Of domestic chore
And drudgery.
The beautiful knowledge
That she was just there.

Used to.

I used to argue
I used to fight
because I loved her and thought it worth
fighting for,

But now I am silent.

Love again

Love. I write in prayer,
over and over the words...
Uttered soundless to a wistful void.
I wish for the courage to confess.
The restraining fear supplanting.
Bending.
My mute, deplorable
ineloquent tongue.
Collapsed under weight of words I fear to speak.

Finally awake

I was awake
most of the night,
until the sun crept over the neighbour's roof,
and yellow orange rays lit dust motes on their
journey to the floor.

I shouldn't entertain the memories of you;
But sometimes they play irresistible,
against the screen of my closed eyes;
And sleep is elusive.

I don't fight it
I revel in it.

In those moments
I don't want to sleep
I would rather replay the sweep of your hand
through your hair
Over and over
Than wake refreshed for the new day.

Grief will do that to a man.

The safest place

You.
A wild untameable shore
Upon which I willingly wrecked my ship;
Drowning crew and captain alike.
Siren singing,
me floundering on;
Lurching drunken to a desolate waterfront.
Bereft of nought but chaotic storms,
and sharp stones jagged under water softened
feet.
No hiding place from chill water blown on
contrary winds.
No boulder to hide my naked heart behind.
Nor shelter to warm my chilled skin.

Until on fighting through,
finding the centre of the storm
a place of calm relief
ringed with hostile promise.
The safest place
Found in any heart.

Fall

In those moments
When I let fall the busy chaos
Of striving
Of making
Doing
You are here
In every spare thought unbidden
Along with my yearning,
to see you again
To renew my fading memories.
to watch you breathe
hear your voice
get lost in your eyes
See your appreciation,
when I bring you a cup of tea.
Have you steal a chip from my plate
Whilst distracting me with your crooked smile.
simple things.
Just you.
It was always you.

How do we live?
When the ones we love are dead.

Compromise is the beginning of the end.

Never compromise on love.
It's the most important thing
That you will ever find or give.
It will bring you most of your joy,
And contentment,
And most of your sorrow.
So to live well
love well.

You won't always love me
Not like this
But I hope you will always remember
What it was like to love me.
As you do today.
When all you required
Was to be next to me.

Missing

I still think of her every day
2 years now
I can't forget
nor want to.

To never hear her voice again.
That is my greatest sadness
It was like listening to the taste of very
expensive wine.
Thankfully her voice fills a decanter in my
head.
Though it is a mere shadow of the reality
I am grateful for even that.
Occasionally I pour myself a glass
just to listen once again.

My disconnected soul

hard to feel the river of joy today,
as though I have disconnected my soul
and went wading on a muddy bank.
Which stole my shoes and left me squelching for
the grassy shore.

It was the moment you imposed the restrictions
and my choice to stay despite.
Though how long that will last I can not say.

I wish

I wish I was writer enough
to pour the words from my soul.
But where to begin
with the ineffable person that is you?
I am paralysed
between fear and awe.
Fear of losing you,
and awe that you even exist.

Never together

We were never together.
Not in any way
the world might call love
or relationship.
But god you made my heart sing
And my soul dance.

Silence

She gave me silence.
It was worse than any words she could have
uttered.
Cut more deeply
left scars which never healed.
It still rings in my ears.

Part of the dead

Part of me died that day.
Electric paddles and norepinephrine
won't wake this corpse.
It's gone.
I saw how you see me
and my vision will now always be clear.

did you contemplate it afterwards?
did you consider my reaction?
did empathy bend your neck?
did realisation hang your head
a dead weight upon your chest?
Or did you just...
Think...
You...
Had...
Won.

True enough

I think it is true to say
I have a fire in me
Which burns all the brighter because of you.
I don't need you to love me
My love exists anyway.
I can't see it going out
And even if you did reject me
It's not like I need you to return my love.
It is
And that is all.

Madness

There is madness
In my heart
Straining to burst upon the world
Restrained by fear of the chaos and destruction
a love so wild would cause.

I couldn't have you

I couldn't have you
So I tried pushing you from my mind
But it didn't work.
You became an intense longing.
Stronger than before my failed experiment.
When I thought the grief
of not having you would break me,
I let you in instead.
No more fight
No more need
No more pain.
Accepting what I would never have.
Allowing you to be,
a kind and generous thought.

And now you are here in my mind
A non-reciprocal love
Which never needs to be fulfilled
Because it is anyway
Can't be made more
Cant be unmade
Is not reliant on you or your acceptance
It is like the gift we give

Not caring for thanks
Or something given in return

My love is,
And that is enough.

Smile

I will always have a smile for you
even on my worst days
I can't help but smile at your impact.
If you knew
how your presence is a burning light in my
being
filling me with warmth.
Even when you are sad, fearful, or angry,
just being near you is enough.
I can easily be without food for a day
A week,
yet, I cannot be without you.

The trouble is

The trouble is,
when the fighting stops
we don't know what to do
you have nothing to say
I have no way to break the silence
but we stay together
like faithful hounds
despite the unfathomable shit we put ourselves
through.
Can you tell me honestly, why are we still
together?

Another kind of death

This is worse by far
to remove your love
Your affection
one molecule at a time.

To hold the hope of reconciliation
but just out of reach.
To allow the chill wind to
pass between us
with no coming together to warm our bodies
the expected end would have been easier
to have grieved and said goodbye
this protracted death is worse by far.

Why I love you

Somehow
When you are with me
I know I am enough
You don't say it
But I know.
It's not what you add
You don't complete me
I just am.
Perhaps
Because I look at you
And know you are too.
Just as you are
Nothing added
Just you

Diagnosis

God the pain.
when she told me
I went cold,
then half slumped,
half sat on the floor.

I couldn't breathe
all I could think...
a world without you
what a desolate place.

My tears came
time and again
as though the endless stream
was tapped
never to be sealed again.
An ocean. And intermittent numbness.
To never see you again
to never look into your face
experience your smile
to never again watch you as you watch the
sunset
looking, looking.
To never touch you
or pull you close
or have you wake me when you are scared.

My soul is torn
and still, you are here
for a short time at least.
businesslike I pull myself together.
hold it in for the end.

but inside we both know
That is what this is.

How can you be so calm?

Love through a face mask.

I would say we find the best things
When not looking
When least expected.
Stumble across a beautiful curiosity.
But you are not a thing to be possessed.

Still...
It wasn't planned
I wasn't looking for someone
I couldn't help myself
You were just there
With your face mask on
And those deep dark eyes gripping me
Pulling me in.

I knew you were
Someone extraordinary
From the first moment I saw your eyes smile.

I stepped into them,
tried to find your soul.

Then you spoke
And your voice melted my limited resistance
Soft, warm, intelligent, powerfully resonant.
Your words left an indelible mark
Which can never be removed.
I have wanted you ever since.

More beautiful still,
I trust you with me.
The parts I fear to show
The parts that hurt
My vulnerable underbelly.
I trust you with those,
Implacably.

Something's are not planned
Some things are just inevitable.

Meeting you is one of the few things that made
life worth living.

Courage

The greatest virtue, all others pale beside;
All backed and driven,
as though without they fail,
a guttering half-hearted light
struggling to reach even the brightest eyes.

Love then, without courage behind its veil?
All dependency.
Great love in contact,
through vulnerability,
must accept the end writ large
In days to come, to tear with rending tears your
thou from your heart.
For if you love, with courage,
inevitable ends will create for you a void of
unimaginable pain,
yet fill before your moments with contentment
so rich,
your breast cannot contain.

Afraid of love

I am not afraid of love
I am in love
I have love
At times I feel I am love.

I am afraid that if I tell her
I will lose her
That is a terrible thought.
But worse still
If she said yes
How much worse would my fear become?

The thought of losing her.
I would be consumed by it
and never sleep again.

So I choose silence.

Just another fantasy

I miss you
The fantasy of you
At times like this.
Imagining a life in which I am wanted.
In which I am not bound by insecurity
Mine or another's.

These last few days I think of you often
Wish you would call
Imagine how I would feel
Enlivened, supported, together,
so simple act,
so efficacious.
But it is a fantasy
a game played only for my mind
to soothe my hurting ego
whilst making myself the victim once again.

wine song

Is there a wine more heady than you?
I drank in the soft velvet depth of your voice,
I fell into the moonless dark of your eyes.
I listened spellbound to the thoughts from your
beautiful mind.
I forgot to breathe
how to speak
There was no world
All but you receded.
You
The one bright figure
In a vista fogged grey and lifeless.
I let myself drown
The most glorious beautiful death.

These rusty bars

These rusted bars of expectations sown
no longer restrain my sorrow,
nor the pain or rage from wasted years on
years.
Unbidden they burst upon the barren plains
beyond
chaos rampant in their wake
debris charred and torn
from bridges burned
dreams shattered.
Merging now
with dulled reality
settling ash
choking smog
in muddy wash.

I blunder to my knees
jarred bones reminding me
I am not dead.
Racks of shuddered conflict burn
from every shamed and fetid pore
Whilst clouds of Corvid black the sky
shrieking chorus to my cries
through field of smoke.

Then stillness.
Settles to my tears
flowing a continuous stream
washing creamy tracks on cheeks
soot blackened.
As gravel dents my knees
and breath comes a ragged wheeze.
My body, limp with fatigue
the collapse of tension
The hopeless sense
Of inevitability,
Snot languidly slips to the ground
Unrepentantly sanctioned.

I called it love

We looked at each other
Felt the pull
Gave to the tug
Let ourselves fall
We called it love.
Did we?
No
That's a fabrication
We didn't call it love

I called it love
Silently.
I never knew what you called it.
Us.
We played with words
A sparing in the space between
You adjusted your hair.
Which you had changed
For me.
No, that's a fabrication
I hoped;
Wished, the effort was for me.
I laughed at your wit
We talked through a hot afternoon
We called it love
No. I called it love.
I have to remember
Remember
It was only me who called it love
And even then
In silence.

Art Gallery

I was lost in fantasy
Whilst reading another's poems.
My mind wandered from the page to you
An imaginary date
In an art gallery.
I said, let's play a game.
Most of these pictures will bore you
some will be interesting.
But one will grab you, pull you in.
I'll watch you, and guess which it is...
Ok you replied.
Ok.. I heard your voice in my head
So simple...
Ok.
It sounded so much like you.

I can't really remember you.
I try,
to keep you alive.
It's been too long.
Vague recollections hover in peripheral vision.
Just out of reach.
And I am frustrated, saddened I cannot grasp
them,
Pull them to me.

But occasionally, I hear your voice, as clear as day
Calling to me from the past
As though you were standing here
Not two feet from my ear.

Power, potential and growth

There can be no growth without pain. No growth without change. Trying to stay the same, demands a stale life, but growth requires the occasional pruning and reshaping in order to flourish. Taking responsibility for our own growth, our own potential, and for creating the best life we can live, means facing challenges with courage and determination. It means not shrinking from distress, but breathing into it and going through. It means we allow change. Allow ourselves to fall apart, collecting those pieces and lovingly putting them back together. Above all, it means taking responsibility for who we are, and this always requires that we become aware of our isolation.

Torn in contradiction

Exactly as you are
Your confidence
Your quick mind.
Easy to love;
Nothing to dislike.
I am afraid.
I want you to grow,
but not away from me.
I want you to fulfil all your potential,
But there is so much potential!
I am greedy.
For you,
exactly as you are.
But I long to see your extraordinary flight.

laugh

Should I laugh less?
Would you ask me to not express my joy,
my excitement?
yet you ask me to suppress tears
should I not feel moved?
Though you can not tolerate my sadness.
Always I should
or don't do this or
don't be that.
but I am both my laughter and my tears.
If I sit on one
I must squash the other also.
I would rather have both in abundance.

Perfectly broken

I am awestruck;
How you, so injured, are yet so perfect.
The world sees your cracks
your stress lines;
Judges you for not being who they expected you
to be.

I just marvel at how you have put yourself back
together.
And more,
That someone who has been shown so little love
Or given love cowed with conditions
Has so much love to give
And does so freely.

There is a beauty in your brokenness
Which once seen could never be forgotten.

Apology

Don't apologise,
not for being you.
Not for being more than you once were.
Not for the soaring thoughts you inspire,
In me,
or anyone.
You are you,
And we are spellbound.

Symphony

I am a symphony of frustration.
Chaos and destruction
expression internalised
mute fascination.
Turning inward
what needs be turned outward.

There is rage, and fear combined
Conflated to the point of pain.
To allow myself to be
When I am not acceptable as I truly am.
I long for,

and run from,
acceptance.

Dyslexia

Dyslexia plays me like a fiddle.
Leaves my sentences censored,
uninhabited.
Missing words I can not hope to spell;
For which spell check can find no solutions
to the salad of letters I thoughtfully presented
its algorithm.
Interlopers insinuate their way into the gaps.
Not conveying the meaning required in the
brevity or strength longed for.

I am cursed;
To walk Blake's Forrest, fleeing proverbial
tigers.
A thick brier of words unintelligible.
A hot shame turning anger rich and clear
for the teachers who thought me stupid.

I think in pictures, not words
So why the fascination with an alien form?

Grace

There is a grace about you
long overlooked
by people who could see nothing
but themselves.

Shedding their idea of you
leaves your grace
unfolding into a world which needed you
though never knew its need.

Defence

You let your defensive self fall away
and compassion took its place
humbling me
and all who knew you.

Afraid of your dark

You are scared by the dark places,
where you fear to look.
Afraid of the grasping roots,
afraid to water them.
To explore their twisted paths.
But you are also the glorious tree
spreading in the light.
Nurturing with your fruit.
Neither part could be
without the other.
No tree can stand the storm
Without roots deep set in the shadows.

Hard work and tears

There are no secrets;
Not here.
Here we work hard.
We cry, allow grief to wrack our bodies
find joy in small things;
In the most unusual and unexpected places.
Laugh in wonder as the broken parts of us
come back together.
Delightful light shining,
through the cracks others have rendered.

You called it love

You didn't need my love
you needed my understanding
to find your love for yourself.
It was this which helped you
reveal the broken parts.
The healing took care of itself.

Let go

When you allowed me in,
trusted me
let ego rest and vulnerability become your
sister
that was the moment I knew
you would be OK,
everything would be alright
no matter what happens next.
Change or no change.
You got out of your own way.
You found your own wisdom
and let go of mine.

Great expectations

It was in letting go
of your expectation
that I would provide the answers.
That you found the path for yourself.
My job was just to refuse to give my answers
which would have confused and mislead.
To not give in to your expectations.
Holding your hand as you take your first steps,
in defining your own solutions,
to the questions you pose.

King

Inconsiderate, unflinching dispassionate.
An uncaring expanse.
Into which we throw our feeble prayers
in arrogant thought that we small things
might change the mind of this vast beast.
But there is no onlooking benevolent or
malevolent
King.
Just cold hard unchangeable indifference.

You said

You said if you let yourself fall apart
You could never come back together.
Yet look at you now,
all bold and brave.
Giving yourself where you are respected.
Holding back where you are not.

You are more together now
after falling to pieces
than you ever seemed before.
I am the privileged witness,
To your beautiful reconstruction.

A little too nice

don't be nice
or good!
Why follow another's should?
If the anxious part of you were to speak
you may find that good exterior becomes a wolf
and expletives erupt from your fanged snarling
mouth
and the world would be better for it.
To see the real authentic you unfettered from
the should of others.

Be free
let the goodie-goodie go.

Never nice

There is no nice
forget that
be respectfully powerful
Wise and grounded.
Filled with passion.
Assertive to your bones.
But, never nice.

What is left

If I let go of my past hurts
what will I have left?

*Less to carry? I hope you will fill this rooom
with hurts from the past, let them fall as you
might the dirt from your boots.*

I wonder what would be left though? Without
these things I carry, what would I be.

Shrugs... "Free?"

shoulds

she never really fit
her coat of expectations;
Or the mass of shoulds on her shoulders.
She was her own indomitable spirit
refusing to be cowed by any of them.

Inside out

Beauty radiates from inside
As we are all a little broken
There are enough cracks for the light to escape.
There is no beauty without imperfections.

Traveller

I am a traveller
From one exotic place to another
Without leaving my chair
No real-world location
No boats, no jet planes
Just one heart to another.

Will not

Wouldn't slow
Wouldn't stop
The endless toil of distraction
Of thoughts washing up, on the shore of his
waking
Mind, and the traumas he tried to drown.
Breaking surface;
Gasping one last breath.
Over and over;
To haunt his waking moments
as much as his sleep.

meaning

when I am busy,
Preoccupied,
with work
with stress and strain
pulled to and fro.
I like to imagine I have spare time
that I will paint and draw
think grand thoughts
write that book.

But when time allows I want none of these
things. It was a ruse
to get me through the storm.

All I really want is you
but you are not mine to have.
And even that may be another ruse,
another meandering diversion
from life's unknowable course;
Or the responsibility of living it.

Mad as a box of frogs

part of me has always been mad
lost in thoughts creative.
Smile through what others studiously avoid,
unfettered by life's usual trappings.
Content to sit and watch the sunrise until it
sets
to enjoy the feel of the breeze against my skin
to allow my mind to race across worlds unknown
ideas falling in and out of consciousness.

Occasionally I grab onto one
that's when the fun starts
pouring myself into every nook
pulling apart and reconstructing
digesting and assimilating, then
in an act of pure defiance
formalising it as art.

Then it is gone.
Leaves my mind,
the figure dissolved
Expunged
leaving a shadow of experience
from which will arise a new spark to draw my
attention

a bright butterfly flitting across my vision
until I reach out to touch its soul
and pour mine into it again.

She

She didn't need approval
She just allowed herself to be
And that made her beautiful
From the inside out.

So, so close

I came so close today
so close to asking
I accepted my fate like a ship meets a thick fog
and stopped moving with any certainty
then sheepishly withdrew altogether.
Always the concern,
another's judgement.
Misunderstanding
or maybe complete understanding.
Better the isolation I have
and the fantasies contained,
than nothing at all.

The longing hangs
Unfulfilled
a drunken sailor marooned in his bottle
awaiting the djinn
impossible made possible
responsibility given purposefully away.

Close is not the same as doing.
How much potential should I waste?
On someone who does not see me as I am.
And will this cowardice ever end?

Beautiful contradiction

It is a beautiful contradiction
to blame you for the way I feel.

Relinquishing my responsibility,
for staying,
and not acting.
You were all instinct
fostering your insecurities
as though they can not be challenged or laid
aside.
The very same I avoid inflaming.
Walking eggshells, in bare feet.
My quiet disappointment attests that
I have no way out.
Or, the way out seems more fraught than staying
put.
I burned those options with astonishing ease.
Whilst attempting to escape other chaos.

And, I can not turn back on,
that which was extinguished,
by your wish to limit me.
when you sought to make me less than I am
or could be.

Words unspoken

the words left unspoken
say more of my fear
of loss and grief
and avoidance of pain
Than any of my tepid excuses could convey.
I used to think it was love
hold the words
spare the person.
But, I wonder now,
Was I just afraid of responsibility?
And, the isolation it brings?

Clarity

There is no meaning and almost no clarity
yet these are the things I seek every day
The part of me that would have meaning
looks endlessly and finds none.
And the part of me that would have clarity;
well it looks at the meaningless lives we live
and wonders how we don't see how meaningless it
all is.

The only clarity I find, is that it is all
meaningless
except for the meaning we ascribe
to meaningless acts.
What a terrible clarity to have.

The real you

It can be a hard thing
to be you
the real you
no roles played
no facades presented
and face others' disapproval and rejection.
but you are you, not some spurious made-up
thing
designed to please the whims of others.
Be your beautiful self
and let the world marvel at your courage.

Old story retold.

I opened a note pad
28 years old,
found I am still the same
I thought I was changed
yet here I am
still wrestling with the same issues
the same insecurities
feeling misunderstood, feeling unseen
self isolation, Not fitting in
... playing the victim
that part is new
to my eyes at least
and maybe the how
of staying stuck for all this time.
Easier to blame them for my misfortune
my isolation
my sadness.
Than to take the reins,
tame the bucking horse.

On waiting

Always, the task of a generation.
To fill itself
with thoughts
and breathe
Supporting the action to come.
A new exploration each moment
that the moment when it comes
upon us may not be wasted
or an interruption
unwanted.

But oh the time wasted
on cliché
the weather, your job, my job, how much this cost
or that.
How the kids are doing so so well
and isn't it grand?
This trivia
that trivia
nothing of interest punctuating existence
as though just being
is a crime to be avoided on pain of death
and what a death!
Death by interminable incipient
Boredom.

That thing

that place in me that births words from
pictures
the force of expression
the images pressing in my head
aching to be expressed
to spill from the brush tip onto the canvas
my need
my desire
is fed by my solitary nature
in solitude my mind comes to life
wakes a million pallets of brilliant colour
spewing them into the world.
All this rejuvenated, By time spent with you,
not in solitude, not at all.

Trying to be normal

Your trying to be normal
Trying to fit in
But I see all sorts of interesting things
Just slipping out the cracks
And as you squeeze harder to keep it contained
More is forced between your fingers
Like playdough in a child's hands.
Be you
Know that normal isn't up to much
It's full of routine
Easy to be alongside
But not much interest
No challenge to the status quo
And yet
All those other bits that slip out unawares
Those are the parts I really want to meet.

Constricted

We live lives small, constricted.
Wondering when it ends
never letting it begin.
Death comes sooner
or later;
Sooner,
later.
As though it matters
when we live lives so small,
so devoid of life.

Acceptance

There is a freedom
Called acceptance
Of what is
The now.
The how of my being
Allowing what is felt
Experienced now
Without trying to change it.
Letting it change itself.

Delighted premonition

Delighted premonition
the end is nigh.
Constraints and fetters
shed to the wind
no more to bend
my shape to yours.
An unprincipled act of faith
to know I am enough
despite what you need me to be.
My heart is free.

No longer treading water
watch me race and fly
as bonds fall
like my final words
to the stony ground.
No more restricted
by the shoulds
poured into my ears
like molten lead
by generations past
to set me deaf to the truth.
That your need for me
to be more than I am
was there to protect that part of you,

that damaged child.
Those children needed someone
to help with their plans
and say "you are just fine",
"Ok as you are ."

.

The void

All of us have a void. It is the part of our authentic self which was never fully accepted, never recognised; Or never allowed to be by significant others. It is not a real void of course, just an abstract conceptualisation of our longing to be accepted. It might or might not be a parent, it could be a friend, a lover, a grandparent, or a teacher. Anyone of significance who couldn't accept part of us, will have left a hole, an impression of us as unacceptable.

If people have a parent-shaped hole in their psyche, it can only be filled by the person they needed to fill it when they were younger. The void was created by the inaction, or action; Their lack of attention, and their lack of ability to be the parent/friend/mentor/lover, we needed; waiting for them to complete this task is a fruitless task, it didn't happen then and it won't happen now. No one else can fulfil this task either, I alone fill that hole in me and recognise it was their lack not mine, or it remains a void. Only you can fill the gaps in you. Not your partners, not your friends. You.

More: A conversation with the void.

More, always more
I never seem to get enough.
Of her
Or anything she brings.

Speak to me from the empty place

I am a never-ending void
I suck insatiable
Never full
I am devourer

And from the place of need

I want to be held
Understood
Seen
Distress dissolved
Void bridged.
I want her to touch me;
as though I am all that matters.

Does she have a name?

Mother dear...

more?

Cold
Hostile,
Distant...
Preoccupied.

Absence

I was lost,
You reached out
I clung to your hand.
Relief a flood through my veins.
A desperate lifeline
My connection to humanity;
The one
Thread
Home.
Defeating the labyrinthian chaos,
The psychotic miasmic thoughts.
A willing touch,
offered, not requested.
And not offered from duty,
arising from desire.
The one thread home.

Awaking from the dream
Like a drowning man breaking surface
For one last gulp of air
The maze still intact
Your hand unproffered
No map home
Hopes scattered like dead children
suspended in my frigid wake.
A Macabre, terrible landscape of the dead.
Meandering isolated.
Past fields sown with seeds of your cold
hostility.
Temple pillars erected to your indifference;
strewn across plateaus of shapeless fear
between.

This was where my madness took me..
To my need for love.
And it's total absence.

Him/male

I see him
Looking past his phone
I feel his surreptitious gaze
Insects scattering across my skin
A cold prickling wave on a hot hot day
As I wonder is he taking photos?
Is he filming me?
My impotence tells me
I can not find out
I am told this world is free
My shame repeats my mother's words
Complicit
You should not have worn that dress
You're leading them on.
What do you expect
Going out dressed like that.
In my anger
Darkly repressed
Turned in upon myself
All joy in the day cast to my shadow
I will go home
And through soft saline Pearls
Cut another sleeper
On the train track up my arm.

Things left unsaid. Steven Eserin 2023

Do you know how it is?

Do you know how it is?
To feel the hungry eyes undress you
To be the cause
For wearing that dress, those shorts
For having a body
To be blamed for another's actions.
Thoughts
Reduced to parts
Sold on the open market
Just by walking in the high street
Wearing, heaven forbid! A skirt.
Can you?
Have you?
Felt fear and loathing
Mingled in darkness
Where bad intent lingers
With lascivious murmur
Unconscious, unthinking
Clammy and vile
directed at you?

Always

I needed you to be the ever there
When I was rocked by fears
To stand
Lean against me
Silently whisper to my soul
I am here
Always.

But you were always mute,
And I learned to flee.

The long path home

A thousand paths
trod in earnest
away from your pain.
To lovers and joy
to sensuous delights;
Pleasure and chaos.
Always avoiding the path,
the one that brings you home.

Projection

I am afraid
that this is just a projection
that you are a screen
upon which I cast my desire for acceptance
total understanding
Love.
And that as illusion
it will fade.
Disappear when I meet the real you.
The authentic being beyond the screen.
The wizard at the end of the road.
I don't want you to be an idea
the shadow cast by the monument I built
dedicated to what I never had.

But, I have to find out.

Acceptance

You are looking for another's acceptance,
you can not accept yourself.
Find excuses to rely on the other.
Giving them responsibility for your value.

It is not their job. It never was.
They may not accept you,
and that will not be about you at all.
Responsibility, so great a cost
to accept the separation it brings.
We accept ourselves
that we might be able to meet others without the
need for their acceptance.
Then if and when acceptance comes
it is the cherry on the cake.
Not necessary,
just a beautiful tasty addition.

Busy

I was busy
didn't respond to your text
and you are outraged because what?
I didn't meet your expectation?
I should have responded... sooner?
But I was holding myself together
trying to breathe
trying not to fall apart
trying not to drown in my own anxiety
My thoughts were chaotic
Racing.
I couldn't keep up
The bottle screamed
Take me! Take me, just fucking take me!!
My reeling mind said DO IT..
Push the fuckit button.
It was all I could do to resist.
So, no I didn't text back
not you or anyone
nor emails
or letters
and I didn't pick up the phone.

I was busy.

Safety in insecurity

you pronounce your insecurities as though the
world must make you safe
but in doing so you censor me.
Your words like manacles
rub raw my wrists and ankles
stifling movement.

In attempting to make yourself safe
you place me under arrest
for crimes I did not commit.
I am mostly just disappointed,
that you and I will never be able to meet
as you fail to see me
beyond the hot fog of your misconception.

I changed

something changed in me
when you placed limits around me,
asked me to be less than I am
less than I wanted or needed to be.
Suddenly my desire for you ran cold.
I am not sure it will warm again.
Which saddens me
for you have been my great love.
I have struggled at times
but have willingly submitted to your bounds
for they have not impacted greatly on mine
But this time. This time I am condemned.
I must stop being me that you might feel OK.
Can I sacrifice that part of me
and still love you?

Importance

I always hoped
I was as important to you
as you were to me.
A big part of me was too afraid to ask
The smaller part hated my cowardice.

In all honesty,
I don't feel worthy of you.
Though it saddens me to say it.
I would not be enough. I'm sure of it.
Not because of your grand expectations
Rather, I don't value what I have to offer.
I am not enough,
then, you feel like more than I deserve.

I feel low

I feel low
simmering through
yesterday's anger
for hours
but mostly unexpressed
now I wonder how to get passed it
but I know what I must do
and you will not like it.
I must be me
and allow those parts you do not like
to exist
to live
and to be free.
If only you could accept me as I am.
I would not be so afraid;
Of a conflict inescapable.

the desert

I stand in the desert
bare feet on the coarse sand
Wild and unproductive
Waiting for rain
Hoping it will sprout some kind of life
Wondering if I can last another day
Or perhaps I am already dead.
I can not feel the wind
The sun
The sand underfoot
The arid dirt caught under my nails
My tongue in my mouth
Or hear my heartbeat
If the rain should come
I shiver with realisation
Fear
I cannot experience it
I will not feel its cool drops trace ragged lines

whilst they race down my face
I long to feel them pool in my jugular notch.
but I am numb.
It, the rain
is outside

I am waiting for life outside
something to transform me
yet there is nothing within
nothing left to transform.

Scorn

There it is again
Casual disdain
Your concerns about things
Not people
Your inability to let people in
Unless they serve to secure your insecurity
What a vast grim repetition
And how ugly it seems
To spend so many years
Chasing the ethereal projection
Of a person who never was
And a need never met.

Sickness calls

As you ask me to be someone else
Brutal rising realisation
From an angry belly
You were never what I thought you were
I fooled myself
In the hope you would be
That thing I never had.

All dust.
Falling through fingers
Scattered by contrary winds
A dream
Now dry as bones
And far more fragile.

Rejection

I long to see her;
Rejection, fear and love in equal measure.
Tranquillity in the storm,
A hope and fear conflated to impasse.
To render inactive any act
That might give an answer.
For then I would have to choose
And god knows I won't do that.

Insidiously present

Funny
How often god comes to mind
Even now
This imaginary friend
Looms in the background
A formidable idea
Personification of blame shifting
Creator of Scapegoats
Ineffectual host.

Time and again

Time and again
You have cut me,
Intended, or no.
Bled either way.
With knives, you forged
To keep old lovers at bay.
That is love, isn't it?
To accept the uncertainty
and The pain
In order to help you heal?
I can't help but feel,
I am losing more blood than you.

Silence seems increasingly attractive

Silence seems increasingly attractive
When words convey too much
Are likely to hurt
Be misunderstood.
Misinterpretation is worse
Almost inevitable
So I rest on my fantasy of what might be
And say nothing.

Lightning rod

She seemed to be made of lightning
Beautiful to watch
Frightening to be close to
Always there was threat
mixed with power and beauty.
Always the knowledge a strike might come
but no predictability at all.
And me? The lightning rod.

Single view restricted.

Lost in linear vision
Encumbered by your self-restricted view
So certain to be right
For fear, perhaps.
Finding patterns in nightmare scenes of your
own creation.
Trying over relentlessly over
to make sense of that which cannot be
understood.
Entwined bracken brier strands of reality
threaded with fantastical thoughts.
Making all seem touchable.
Lending a hint of the real.

Never seeing the delusion
The hideous reality.
You were not chosen
You are not special.
No messenger from a benevolent overseer guides
your path.
No fictional entity set you on this road.
It was random
The universe uncaring, dispassionate
Which before hindsight set your mind
To stringing unconnected things on woven
tapestries of tales;
Didn't care, and still won't.
About your suffering or mine.
But this world you wove from your fiction
Alienates you from your peers
Prevents you from receiving
the very love you need to heal.
You have entombed yourself
In the enveloping fetid brier
And no one has the sword of truth to set you
free.
It is sheathed at your side.

You limit her

You try to limit her
Build a cage around her creativity
Her desires.
So afraid of her free spirit

That you imprisoned her in a cage built of your
insecurity.

All you did was imprison yourself
Now she is gone
And you could have flown with her
But you couldn't see past your pain.
Your own freedom,
lost behind the should of another
The should you used to contain her.

constriction

As soon as you tried to contain her
Her spirit rose up
Pushed against you.
Still, you tried to enslave
Even when she offered you freedom
The choice to go with her
Into the bright dawn.
But you chose your gilded cage
And here you remain
Alone.

There are words

There are words
Hidden beneath the lump in my throat
Tearing me raw
Between letting them out
And keeping them in.
And if they fly
What freedom would they bring
If they fall on stone ears
Then rejection replaces constriction.
Which is worse?
The knowing or the not knowing?
The saying or the silence?

The sea

There is a sea
Vast beauteous
Unknowable depth
unfathomable intricate.

I have stared
But cannot see your depth
I would dive in
But fear I may drown.

I grieve;
The loss,
My impotence,
The never knowing...
And my inability to leave the safety of the
shore.

Cramped

I left your cramped ass behind me
I can't be constrained by your lack of response
one strangled moment longer
I put in vast effort
for what seems like aeons.
Wasted too many precious moments in my life
thinking the fault was mine.
Trying to make you change
when you couldn't
didn't want to.
I only just realised I had it the wrong way
around.

Now I awake
from a restless dream
aware of things changing about me
unsure, as it all seems slightly out of place
but clarity is coming, in waves of recognition.
Aware now, I do not need you to change;
It was not me. I am just fine as I am.
I no longer need your response to know I am.

Dream of death

I am standing in a clearing
the wind moves the leaves of trees around me
and the grass around my feet
Yet I cannot feel it upon my skin
Or fill my lungs.
The stream flows fast, but I cannot hear its
sound
the clouds run from the wind and clear a path
for the sun; But I can not feel it upon my skin,
For I am dead.

Depression

Black,
it hangs
curls
insidious, cloying
with its frigid tendrils
leaving no place unmolested.
Drained of essence
of will
to eat
to breathe.
Just a stubborn heartbeat
remnant of a life longed for
beyond the binding arms of sickly black.

The scapegoat

Thought of lack,
lack of thought
leads to the same excuse
The dream alone
a wish.
Desire,
to be wanted,
seen, touched.
Loved?
Lost in the mire of translation
in blame
in imagined meanings to distant words
compassion gone
lost with the respect
left with the dream alone.

Boundaries

Hot discomfort
truth denied
no rift to swallow underfoot the hapless pair
sat dumbfounded by the unbound lass.
Goods displayed, coquettish to all.
No fear of judgement.
No need to cover
or make amends
for there was no slight.
Always with lack of contact
their discomfort grows.
And under challenge dismiss
leave all
half-revealed
diaphanous bands
desire tucked away out of sight.

light upon your hair

Your words fell upon my ears
as fine hair brushed with the wind.
A fleeting shiver runs from bottom to top
As each sound does its work.
And your smile
like the autumn sun catching golden leaves
on its journey to my skin
as I bask in its soft warmth.

Mother dear

Intoxicated by our toxic attachment
polluted by osmosis
I sweat
and shake the poison from my pores
with cold shivers.
An unholy love
this love of ours.

Depressed

Knowing what lay before me
I awoke
ponderously raise my head
opened my eyes a crack
the light heaving a blow to my mind
forcing defeat again
onto my withered sight
I hide
Again
from the day
slept it away
in the hope things would change
though nothing changes when I do nothing.

I burned those bridges

I burned those bridges intentionally
I warmed myself on the flames
Danced in the ashes
Until I was black from head to toe
In charcoal soot,
I celebrated the burning
Sung its freedom loud as timbers split with
flame
Because I never have to listen to you again
Not your blame
Not your whining victim
Not your gaslighting that never ends.

I dance

free

Saccharin smile

you treat me to a smile
Saccharin sweet with the promise of lust
ill-formed and listing
Running to the drum of a lust one-sided
Which meets me not as a person
But as a thing
A means to an end
A lust incontinent
And once internalised insecurity satiated
If only for a few minutes
I am cast aside

Pretend

I don't want to watch this show
I'm sitting here
Giving away my life
Wasting precious moments
Watching TV
But that's a lie
I'm not watching TV
That's just a role
A game to cover reality
For us both
No, another lie
For me
I can't stand to be in the same room as you
So I am here
Hiding in a virtual world
A TV show
Where the actors are more real than me.
So we don't fight.
And I can pretend
That one day you will forgive me.

Text

I sent you a text
A single word
A question.
"Breakfast?"
And what I meant was
"Love?"
You declined to answer.
This void holds me surrounded
Knowing you
Or anyone else
Are not the answer.
But feeling desire and hope
Mixed with fear.
A trembling frame
Breath shallow
Excitement unsupported.
My fear?
That this yearning will never end.

Roaches

Shame burns me
My tears stream
Against my will
Attempts to brush them aside
To smile through them
As though this will make them disappear

They are cockroaches
Streaming from my eyes
Something to hide
How grim does your house need to be
Before cockroaches take up residence
In the grime
They scuttle down my face
Each one a new hot streak
Reminding me
You do not, can not
Love one such as me.

Like the rats that live
between the walls
I know they are there
I hope never to meet them
Then conspicuous in the dark
I see one slink against the skirting

Another hot rush.

I long for sleep
To anaesthetise my pain
Wish away the day
My life
But no rest comes
No sleep
Rejection bites
As sure as bed bugs crawling
Discomfort and certainty
Of shame and isolation .

Connections made

Hello my boy how are you..

He can't remember my name, but he is glad..
perhaps for a visitor.

Have you seen Tom?

That's his other son, the prodigal one who hasn't
shown his thieving face in years.. "no" I reply,
"not for a week or two, but I'm sure he's
alright."

I get muddled. seems longer. But then at 20 I was
away with the army, didn't give my old man a
second thought.

He's 56 I want to say. Irritated in my bordem.
How I bore myself, with my sense of duty, my
boring job, my boring life... 'well I'm sure he's
ok, it's only a week since we saw him." *The lie*
slips easy from my lips. I know he can't tell.

Silence. *He used to have such an infallible*
memory. He had such a bright intellect. Reduced
to a repeating thought... I wonder if this will
be my fate, to gradually diminish.

I was remembering just this morning, I used to
run machines, back in the war. Making small
brass connectors... Great big machines they were..
to make these tiny little things, smaller than
your finger nail..

He points to his finger, the little one, with the
part blackened nail. He always seemed to have a
part blackened nail. I wonder how he manages it
in a care home.

Have you seen Tom?

I come back from my wandering thought. There he
is, back on track. The same old track. Record
broken and skipping. "Yes" I reply, just this
morning, he said to say hi."

He beams. As the lie lubricates his heart.

I must change my life, I can't live like this, I
am so tired, so bored... And so full of rage... I
begin to hate my indifference.

Connection

There can be no therapy without connection.
Learning to connect is half the battle, and the
area of connection, of unconditional acceptance,
is where the healing begins. There are moments
of profound connection, moments like the I-thou,
where we connect so completely and know each
other so profoundly, we experience what amounts
to a spiritual connection.

The mystery

I think I loved everything about you
Especially the parts I couldn't understand.
The mystery of them drew me further into the
story
until I was lost in your pages.

Few regrets

Few regrets.
Chief among them, that I didn't get more time,
to learn everything there was to know about
you.
That would be a life well spent.

Unwritten

thinking of words to describe you...
how would I write poetry without words?
it can't be done
so I sit in impotent silence
and stare at the blank page in wonder.

Seen

Can you see me?

Do you want to be seen?

You avoided my question...

I did, and I don't yet know. My judgments are not you, my thoughts are not you, and my eyes lie. Can I say I see you? I can say I want to. But do you want to be seen?

No. I think not.

Then I will never meet you, and the part of me that wants to must accept I can not.

You want to?

Yes. To truly meet, that is the greater part of life. Maybe the only part worth living.

I never had that..

What a small life I live.
Safe... but so so small.

Seeing

Some think this game (psychotherapy) a nonsense.
It is no small thing
to allow oneself to be seen
to find understanding in the dark places of our
soul
to explore our shadows
and step from them into light.

To those who take my hand and walk the path,
It makes perfect sense.

Misfit

Tell me something important about yourself?

I'm a bit of a misfit
cheerful on the outside
but my being is sad.
I am not anti-social
but I have few friends..
and I really dislike shallow conversation.
I guess those two might be linked.

Rare

We were talking
in dreams
when I realised with tears rising
that was the piece we were looking for,
I think to myself, "you are done."
And, at the same moment,
you looked up, opened your eyes
stared out of the window and said
"I think I am done"
"*I think you are.*"
exquisite, perfect moment of recognition
seen clearly
experienced fully
Connected.
Broad smile and tears rolling.
How extraordinarily rare.

I thou

We cannot name that immutable ineffable thing
the I thou and the moment of change
Point of connection stretching to infinity.
All words just fall away
none fit
compassion fills the space between
and we are changed.
In that space, I know.
Things I was unaware of
and I see things I could not see
and you also see me,
when we connect.
It is the simplest of intimacies
the intricacy of vulnerability and courage
combined
poured lovingly into the space within and
between
as though we and the universe are one
and there is no expectation
To be anything more than we are.

Muzzy headed

when I said
"I just can't think straight, its all jumbled
nonsense"
you replied.
*"so be with the part of you that can't think
straight, see what it has to say"*
I found that I had a lot to say from that part
and it all made perfect sense..

Gentle curiosity

The gentle curiosity
with which he met the world
not expecting it to change for him,
acceptance of ambivalence,
allowing without forcing.
There was grace in this,
expressed in simplicity
cloaking a complexity
vast and unknowable.

Absurdity

Absurdity of being
vast unknowable
the total lack of meaning;
To a sentient creature looking for meaning.

Thoughts gymnastic bend to make
an act seemingly real.
Or lasting.
Painting meaning for the one
across what has none.
That relief might hold for time enough
to forget inevitable ends
and dream immortal
of times they will never see.

What does she represent?

What does she represent?
I hate that question.
What if I love her because she is extraordinary?
Rather than an ideal she represents for me.
some transference trope.
What if, she is just so spectacularly awesome
I am unable to resist falling for her?
Did you consider that?
She is extraordinary, no one can take that from
her.
Or it seems, from me.

Lips

The great thing about your lips
aside from their uncommon beauty
is that they fit mine perfectly.

Unconditional hug

sometimes I need a hug
the kind of hug that lets me know you really
don't want to let go
the kind where we fit together so perfectly that
I can't bare to separate
because if we do we can never have that moment
again.
I want to feel your warmth
and your unconditional acceptance of me as me
in the knowledge you choose to hold me.

Doubt

I doubt we will speak again
yet knowing you has changed me
in powerful ways
you have been a beautiful lesson
that I would not have lived without.

Solitude

I revel in my solitude
It's where I think
Reframe
coalesce ideas, concepts.
Allow creative exploration
Develop artistic ideas.
It is where I allow feelings to be,
enable experience without interruptions.
Go through and out the other side.
In short, it is where I grow.

If you want to take me from my solitude
Make sure you offer me good company
Or a powerful love.

These are the only other things I live for
besides.

Dance like nobody's watching

She danced like an exploding jellyfish
Not a care who watched
Or what they thought
Just a perfect moment of bliss
Lost in music and the embrace of movement.

You are

You are just like the good feeling
that washes over my tired soul
after a long day of hard toil
when I accomplished everything and more,
feeling content
and ready to rest
bone tired.

You are like that glorious moment of letting go'

of restful contentment.
But, with you It's every time I see you,
every time you speak.

She was the Earth mother

Tough uncompromising love
Eager compassion
Held together by scars
Grounded as ancient trees
Unafraid of her roots
Relentless in her desire to see me whole.

maybe

I barely tolerate reality,
Mostly because you are part of it.
No pressure...
But if you were not,
I might go mad for the lack of you.

I have the best job

I have the best job
I get to meet the most extraordinary people
beautiful and pained
struggling against life's chaos
unable to relinquish control.

We meet, and in the space between we find
contact
in that fertile place we explore where we end
and begin; to allow,
perhaps for the first time
authenticity to arise
and experience the acceptance
of self, as it is.

Every time a client is healed
so is a small part of me.
It's not why I do the job
It is just a beautiful addition.

I work hard
but I often feel I don't work at all.
We create the most exquisite relationships.
It is this that is healing above all else.

More intimate than most people experience in
any other place or time.
Sharing things no one has heard
finding understanding in our shadows.
I am, therefore, in a constant state of semi-
grief.
Not an overwhelming grief
but grief nonetheless.
For the relationships that can go no further
for the people I have helped whom I will never
see again.
It's like watching a butterfly leave the
chrysalis
but never seeing them fly.

I don't get to see them again
after they leave this room
they step away from me
exactly as they should
as there can be no dependence.
And then they are gone.
And I am left with a beautiful mix of awe,
sadness and Joy.

Silence

United in silence
we speak
no words
understanding all.
Thoughts come and go.
In this moment,
not past or future
but running soon to more;
Both elaborate and desperate.
The crying of my heart
witnessed by God
in silence
but understood by you.

Thanks

You have been there
my solidity
my containment.
For this hour a week
you have been constant
when my life has been chaos
a safe space
where everything
all my shit
all my disaster
was accepted
Held
sorted and sifted
given back with love.
What a magical thing,
to find a space like this.

Heart map

I was following my heart
But I don't think it had a map
And now I'm hopelessly lost

Woodwork

I worked the wood
Joint carved
With saw
And mitre
Chisel shaving clean across the grain
Smell of cut oak rising
The hardness of timber
Giving to the bite of plane
Rich wafer shavings falling light
To a sawdust ridden floor.
Softly scrunching under foot

And after hours the chair evolved
From block and spoke to me.
I am good
Well made, strong and beautiful
Graceful but unbreaking
Much like you.

And I
Fulfilled from a days toil
Felt the surety of knowledge
My hands made this
Just as it made me.

Let slip

Let slip the mask
Culture created
The ego dance
Beguiling

Let them fall and look a fresh
Upon your comrade's arms
And let them see
For once at least
The man behind the mask.

You can know me
As the role played dictates
With distance and cliche
Or you can meet me as you
And accept what we are
No need to be more,
Or less.

Awareness

When shoulds abound
The expectation
Of tradition
And long dead peers.
The self so lost
Can see no more
Its self, nor those it seeks.

Awareness lost
Behind the mask,
The one we wore with shame.

For finding here
The one true self
Alive beneath the blame.

Individuality

As hot ember
Falls from grate
It lies aside
Heat dissipating in slow death,
and dead before all energy was spent.

Whilst its brothers in the hearth
Allowing individual authenticity
Within the connected heart
Burn full force. Just as they should
Warming room and hearts and faces
Fuel expended to extinction, bright and hot.
Burning to ash
No life squandered.

Everything dies in isolation.

About the author

Steven Eserin is a Gestalt Psychotherapist who
trained in Ireland at the Irish Gestalt centre.
Graduating in 2002. At the time of writing e has
a thriving private practice on the south coast
of England working with individuals in 1-1
sessions, groups and couples. He is also a
clinical supervisor with supervisees around the
world and a trainer across a wide range of
mental health related subjects. For more
information on personal therapy or to contact
Steven to discuss training or supervision
related matters please visit
www.steveneserin.com

Printed in Great Britain
by Amazon